A Book

Contents

Fun Boats, Work Boats

There are many kinds of boats.

Some are for work.

Some are for fun.

3

Boats for Fun

All of these boats are used for fun.
Some are used for racing.

Going Fishing

Boats are used for fishing.

People fish with nets, rods, and lines.

6

Take a Ride

Sometimes people use boats for getting around.
They even use water taxis!

9

Homes on Water

Some people live in a houseboat.

Their home is on the water.

On Land and Water

Some boats can travel on land.
Some of them have wheels.

A hovercraft travels on a cushion of air.

FIRE ·RESCUE

IRISH HILLS

13

To the Rescue

Sometimes boats and ships
get into trouble.
Rescue boats help them.

A life ring can help save someone who has fallen overboard.

The ship's passengers are doing a lifeboat drill. They are all wearing life jackets.

Index